Dec 18

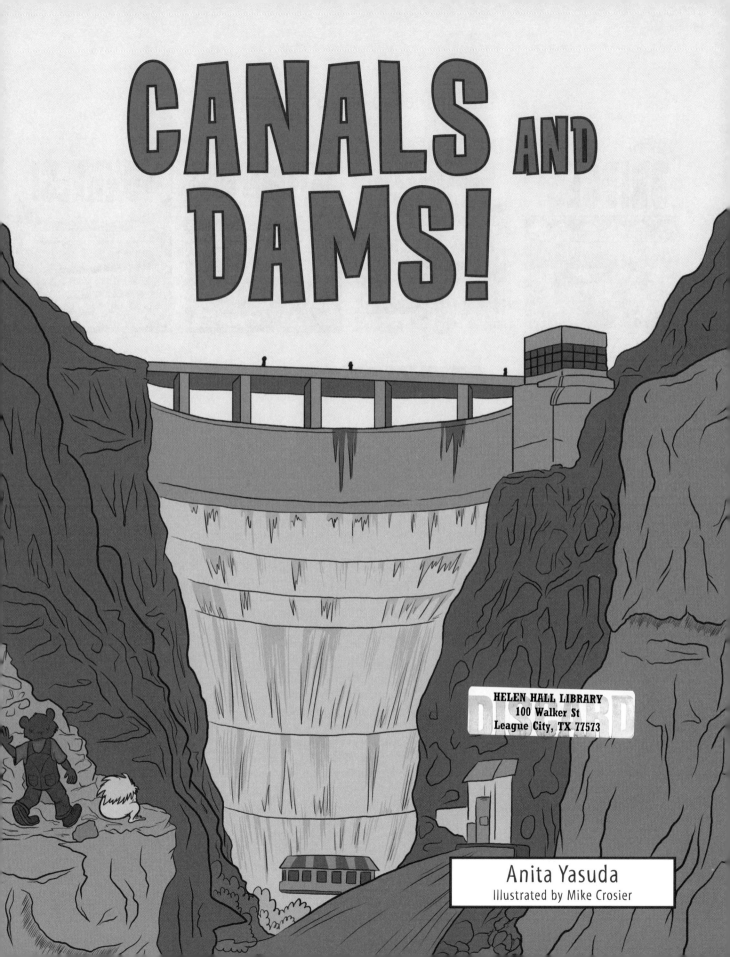

CANALS AND DAMS!

Anita Yasuda

Illustrated by Mike Crosier

Titles in the **Explore Engineering** Set

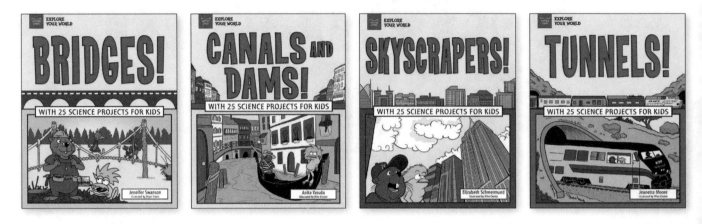

Check out more titles at www.nomadpress.net

Nomad Press
A division of Nomad Communications
10 9 8 7 6 5 4 3 2 1

This book was manufactured by Versa Press,
East Peoria, Illinois
August 2018, Job #J17-12595

ISBN Softcover: 978-1-61930-647-9
ISBN Hardcover: 978-1-61930-645-5

Educational Consultant, Marla Conn

Questions regarding the ordering of this book should be addressed to
Nomad Press
2456 Christian St.
White River Junction, VT 05001
www.nomadpress.net

Printed in the United States of America.

CONTENTS

Interested in primary sources? Look for this icon. Use a smartphone or tablet app to scan the QR code and explore more! Photos are also primary sources because a photograph takes a picture at the moment something happens.

If the QR code doesn't work, there's a list of URLs on the Resources page. Or, try searching the internet with the Keyword Prompts to find other helpful sources.

→ **KEYWORD PROMPTS**

canals and dams 🔍

3000 BCE: Jawa Dam is built in Mesopotamia.

2700 BCE: The ancient Egyptians build one the earliest dams, the Sadd el-Kafara Dam along the Nile River.

1200 BCE–800 BCE: Ancestors of Native Americans build Las Capas in present-day Arizona. This is the oldest canal system in North America.

520 BCE–510 BCE: Persian emperor Darius I builds a canal from the Nile River to the Red Sea.

THIRD–THIRTEENTH CENTURY CE: The Chinese build several dams and canals to prevent flooding and to improve transportation.

FIFTH CENTURY CE: Work begins on the 1,100-mile Grand Canal in China. It is completed during the Sui Dynasty (581–618 CE).

1179–1209: The Naviglio Grande is a canal built to bring marble from quarries to Milan, Italy, for use on a cathedral.

1500: Artist and scientist Leonardo da Vinci invents the mitered lock gate, allowing canals of different levels to be joined together.

1825: The Erie Canal in New York State opens. It connects the Great Lakes to the Atlantic Ocean and opens western states to development.

1869: The Suez Canal joins the Mediterranean Sea to the Red Sea. Cargo ships no longer have to sail the 6,000-mile-route around the tip of Africa.

1642: The Briare Canal in France joins the Seine River to the Loire River. Parts of the canal descend 206 feet in 32 miles.

1718: A system of levees is built to control flood waters along the Mississippi River at New Orleans, Louisiana.

1942:
The Grand Coulee Dam on the Columbia River in the state of Washington opens. It is one of the largest concrete structures in the world.

1942:
The All-American Canal opens along the border between the United States and Mexico. It is the longest irrigation canal in the world, bringing water from the Colorado River to California.

1936:
Work is completed on the Hoover Dam on the border of Nevada and Arizona. The dam harnesses the power of the Colorado River.

1959:
The Saint Lawrence Seaway opens, linking the Great Lakes to the Atlantic Ocean through a series of canals and locks.

1914:
The Panama Canal is built across the Panama Isthmus, linking the Atlantic and Pacific Oceans. Cargo ships no longer have to sail the long route around the tip of South America.

1970:
The Aswan High Dam on the Nile River opens. It creates a 300-mile-long reservoir called Lake Nasser.

FUTURE:
When finished, the Rogun Dam in Tajikistan will be the tallest dam in the world at 1,263 feet tall.

1902:
The first Aswan Dam on the Nile River is completed. For its time, the dam is a marvel of engineering.

1982:
Built by Brazil and Paraguay, the Itaipu Dam on the Paraná River opens. The dam is one of the largest hydroelectric dams in the world.

2003:
Three Gorges Dam across the Yangtze River in China begins operating. It is the world's largest hydroelectric dam.

INTRODUCTION

LET'S EXPLORE CANALS AND DAMS

Have you ever traveled down a river in a boat? Rivers are very useful for getting people and things from one place to another. But what if there is no natural river flowing where people and things need to travel? One solution is to dig a canal!

A canal is a manmade channel of water. Often, you'll find canals working together with dams. Canals and dams are both structures that change the flow of water. This is useful for transportation, producing electricity, and getting water where it's needed.

1

Canals and dams often work together as part of a system. One allows water to flow and the other stops water from flowing.

Have you ever heard of the Hoover Dam? This dam supplies 1.3 million people in Nevada, Arizona, and California with electricity. It sends water to people hundreds of miles away. It's as tall as a 60-story building! The Hoover Dam is an engineering marvel that is part of a system of canals and dams that allowed many of the great cities of the American Southwest to grow and thrive.

WHAT ARE CANALS?

A canal is built to move water from one place to another or to connect two bodies of water. Why would you want to do this?

Sometimes, people live far away from the water they need. Canals can bring water to farms, which can be used for irrigation to grow crops. Farm animals also need water. Canals can bring water to cities so people living there have water to drink and bathe in.

THE ALL-AMERICAN CANAL (CREDIT: CHARLES O'REAR, NATIONAL ARCHIVES)

For example, water from the Colorado River is brought by the All-American Canal from the Imperial Dam in Arizona to California's Imperial Valley. The valley has some of the most important farmland in the state. Approximately 75 different types of crops are grown there.

If you have a sip of tap water at the Disneyland Resort in Anaheim, California, it might have come from the Colorado River. Or it might have traveled all the way from the north of the state through a system of canals.

Canals are also built to link two bodies of water. This can make it easier for ships to get from one place to another. Before the Panama Canal was built in 1914, ships had to travel thousands of miles all the way around the tip of South America.

CANALS AND DAMS!

Going around South America was the only way to get between the Atlantic Ocean and the Pacific Ocean. Now, using the Panama Canal, ships can cut across Panama, traveling the 48 miles in just 8 to 10 hours.

WHAT ARE DAMS?

A dam is an incredibly useful type of wall. It slows or holds back the flow of water. A dam is usually built across a river or a stream. As the dam slows the water down, an artificial lake forms behind it. This lake is called a reservoir.

A reservoir is like a giant bowl. Unlike the bowls in your kitchen, reservoirs can hold billions of gallons of water.

4

What can you do with all this water? Lots of things. You can build a canal to move some of it to where you need it! Or enjoy boating and swimming in it. The water held back by a dam can even be used to make electricity.

A dam can be one of the biggest structures in the world. It must be strong and stable to resist the forces pushing and pulling on it. The weight and flow of water is a force that pushes against a dam. Gravity is a physical force created by the earth that pulls down on the dam. If a dam doesn't resist these forces, it will collapse.

force: a push or a pull that causes a change of motion in an object.

gravity: a force that pulls objects to the earth.

collapse: to fall in or down suddenly.

engineer: someone who uses science, math, and creativity to solve problems.

WORDS ⊕ KNOW

BEAVER DAM

Most of the dams we'll read about in this book are constructed by people, but humans are not the only ones who make dams! The American beaver is a busy engineer famous for its dam-building skills. Beavers build dams out of trees, branches, twigs, and mud to turn streams into ponds. In Wood Buffalo National Park in Alberta, Canada, the largest beaver dam in the world is approximately 2,790 feet long. That is twice the length of Hoover Dam, or roughly the length of nine football fields! The dam is so large that it can be seen from space.

You can see the official Parks Canada video showing this enormous dam at this website.

KEYWORD PROMPTS

Canada beaver dam video 🔍

← – — ⌐

CANALS AND DAMS!

CANALS AND DAMS ARE EVERYWHERE

Canals and dams are built all over the world. In fact, people have built canals and dams in six of the seven continents (Asia, Africa, North America, South America, Europe, and Australia).

In this book, you'll discover what canals and dams are, why we build them, and how they impact people and the environment. You'll learn about how engineers approach problems by using the engineering design process to find solutions. You'll even use the engineering design process to work on your own engineering projects!

The book will also share some cool facts. Some dams are giant mega structures. They make the pyramids of Egypt look small. These super dams stand as tall as skyscrapers!

You will also read about the earliest, largest, and most important canals and dams in the world. Some of these record-breakers are in the United States. One might be near you!

Ready? Grab your hard hat—there are canals and dams to explore!

WHAT DID THE BEAVER SAY TO THE TRE

HA HA HA HA

It's been nice gnawing yo

DID YOU KNOW?

There are more than 57,000 big dams all around the world! Lots of planning goes into a dam.

GOOD ENGINEERING PRACTICES

Engineers and scientists keep their ideas organized in notebooks. Engineers use the engineering design process to keep track of their inventions, and scientists use the scientific method to keep track of experiments.

As you read through this book and do the activities, record your observations, data, and designs in an engineering design worksheet or a scientific method worksheet. When doing an activity, remember that there is no right answer or right way to approach a project. Be creative and have fun!

Engineering Design Worksheet
Problem: What problem are we trying to solve?
Research: Has anything been invented to help solve the problem? What can we learn?
Question: Are there any special requirements for the device? What is it supposed to do?
Brainstorm: Draw lots of designs for your device and list the materials you are using!
Prototype: Build the design you drew during brainstorming. This is your **prototype**.
Results: Test your prototype and record your observations.
Evaluate: Analyze your test results. Do you need to make adjustments? Do you need to try a different prototype?

Scientific Method Worksheet
Question: What problem are we trying to solve?
Research: What information is already known?
Hypothesis/Prediction: What do I think the answer will be?
Equipment: What supplies do I need?
Method: What steps will I follow?
Results: What happened and why?

ENGINEERING NOTEBOOK

Leonardo da Vinci (1452–1519) was an artist and engineer. Many people know him for painting the *Mona Lisa*. Fewer know that he was also interested in the flow of rivers. He filled a 7,000-page notebook with ideas and drawings! Create your own engineering notebook to write down your research, questions, and ideas.

SUPPLIES

* ✳ 6 standard envelopes
* ✳ glue stick
* ✳ crayons, colored pencils, stickers
* ✳ 24 notecards to fit envelopes (or make notecards from plain scrap paper)
* ✳ scrap paper
* ✳ pencil
* ✳ ribbon or string
* ✳ scissors
* ✳ clear tape

1 Spread out your envelopes in a straight line. Do not glue the first envelope. Place glue on the flap of the second envelope. Press the bottom of the first envelope onto the glue. Continue to glue the envelopes together until they look like an accordion.

2 On the front of the first envelope, use your crayons and colored pencils to add decoration. You can also add stickers. Insert four notecards into each envelope.

3 From the scrap paper, cut out six labels for your envelopes. Use the pencil to write down the chapter headings. Glue one label to each envelope. Decorate them with your crayons or colored pencils.

PROJECT!

4 Cut two pieces of ribbon roughly 4 inches in length.

5 Tape the end of each ribbon to either end of your accordion notebook. You can tie your notebook shut when you are not using it. If you want to make your book larger, simply remove the ribbon and add more envelopes with more notecards.

DID YOU KNOW?

In 1200 BCE, ancestors of Native Americans built canals to carry water from the Santa Cruz River to their fields in what is now Tucson, Arizona, where they grew crops such as maize. Today, a 335-mile canal that begins near Lake Havasu supplies Tucson, Arizona, with 44 billion gallons of water each year.

ESSENTIAL QUESTIONS

Each chapter of this book begins with an essential question to help guide your exploration of canals and dams. Keep the question in your mind as you read the chapter. At the end of each chapter, use your engineering notebook to record your thoughts and answers.

INVESTIGATE!

What problem do you see that you would like to fix? What can you invent to solve it?

PROJECT!

ENGINEER A BEAVER DAM

Beavers are amazing engineers. Do you think that you can build a dam as well as a beaver? This is your chance to try. Design, create, and test your own model of a beaver dam.

1 Place tinfoil on the baking sheet or container. Mold the foil high on the sides. This will allow you to add more water to the experiment.

2 Place your container on a flat surface, inside or outside. Create a dam using sticks, pinecones, and pebbles in the center of the tray. What is the problem you are trying to solve? Take a notecard out of your engineering notebook and set up a scientific method worksheet. Write down what you think will happen when you pour water onto the tray.

3 Next, pour a little water into one end of the tray and observe what happens. Write down your results in your worksheet. How were your results similar or different from your prediction?

* tinfoil
* baking sheet with deep sides or long plastic container
* sticks, pinecones, and pebbles
* plastic jug
* engineering notebook and pencil
* drying cloth
* modeling clay

4 Remove the sticks. Dry your tray with the cloth. Now, rebuild your dam using modeling clay for mud. Write down what you think will happen when you pour water onto the tray.

5 Pour a little water at the top of the tray and observe what happens. Record your results in your scientific method worksheet. How were your results similar or different from your prediction?

TRY THIS! Use the engineering design process to design and build a better dam with some additional natural items, including leaves, bark, and grass. Can you build the dam higher and thicker? Try using more water or building a longer river with tinfoil. Test it outdoors! Keep track of your designs and results in an engineering design worksheet.

FORCES

There are forces all around you. You can't see them, but you can see what they do. Have you ever kicked a ball, used a remote control, or written on a piece of paper? Then you have used push as a force to move the ball, button, or pencil. Have you ever opened a drawer, played tug of war, or put on a pair of socks? You have used pull as a force to move the drawer, a person, and your socks. What are some other ways you use pushing and pulling forces at school and home?

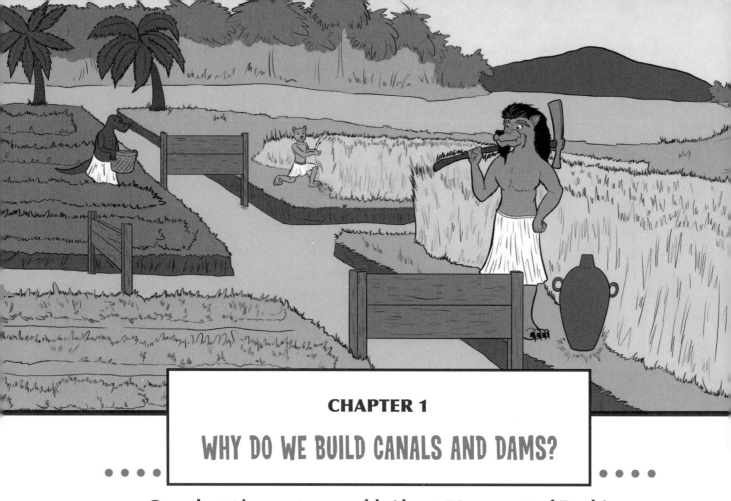

CHAPTER 1

WHY DO WE BUILD CANALS AND DAMS?

Our planet is a watery world. About 70 percent of Earth's surface is covered in water. It's no wonder that Earth has many nicknames describing its watery surface. Have you ever heard Earth called the "Blue Planet" or the "Big Blue Marble?"

Water flows in our lakes, ponds, rivers, and streams. Most surface water is found in Earth's massive oceans. Water also exists beneath your feet. There is moisture in the soil. There is water stored in the spaces between the soil and rock in reservoirs called aquifers. Water can also be found in the air outside, falling as rain, snow, and sleet. Water is almost everywhere!

? INVESTIGATE!

How are canals and dams connected to the world's water supply?

aquifer: an underground layer of water-filled rock.

freshwater: water that is not salty.

WORDS ⊙ KNOW

Thousands of years ago, our ancestors began building systems to control water. They wanted to store water to use when there was too little of it. They wanted to be able to move water to areas where it was too dry to grow crops. They wanted to prevent flooding. Canals and dams helped people achieve these goals.

To understand the purpose of canals and dams, let's take a closer look at the world's water.

WATER, WATER EVERYWHERE

It might seem as though water can be found everywhere on Earth. But water is not evenly spread around the world. And not all of it is usable for humans and other living creatures.

Less than 3 percent of Earth's water is fresh. Freshwater is what every single person must have to live. How many ways have you used freshwater today? Did you brush your teeth or take a shower? Maybe you washed your hands or drank a glass of water with your lunch.

THIS 1972 PHOTOGRAPH OF EARTH FROM SPACE IS CALLED "THE BLUE MARBLE"
(CREDIT: NASA/APOLLO 17 CREW)

water cycle: the continuous movement of water from the earth to the clouds and back to earth again.

glacier: an enormous mass of ice and snow that moves slowly with the pull of gravity.

water vapor: water as a gas, such as fog, steam, or mist.

evaporate: to change from a liquid to a gas, or vapor.

atmosphere: the blanket of gases around the earth.

condense: when a gas cools down and changes into a liquid.

WORDS to KNOW

A WATER DROPLET'S JOURNEY

All of Earth's water is constantly moving on the same cycle—the **water cycle**! Water flows in rivers, ponds, oceans, or hangs out in **glaciers** for 10,000 years before melting or turning into **water vapor**. Heat from the sun causes water in the oceans, lakes, and rivers to change into water vapor. "Here we go!" the tiny water drops say to each other as they **evaporate** and are carried up into the **atmosphere** by warm air.

The temperatures in the atmosphere are much cooler. When water vapor cools, it **condenses** and forms clouds. The clouds get bigger and heavier as more water vapor condenses into water droplets. The cloud becomes so heavy that the water falls back to Earth as rain, snow, or fog. Drip-drop-plop-SPLAT!

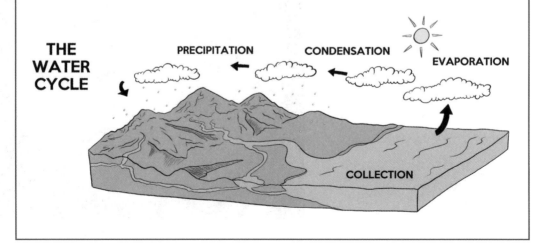

THE WATER CYCLE

PRECIPITATION CONDENSATION EVAPORATION

COLLECTION

People use water every day. They drink, cook, and prepare food with water. They also use water to grow crops. The average person in the United States uses 80 to 100 gallons of water each day.

Most water in the world is saltwater. Saltwater is found in Earth's five oceans. People can't survive on saltwater. It tastes very bitter, and if you drink saltwater, it only makes you thirstier.

One way to get freshwater to people who live in dry places is to build dams and canals to collect water and move it where it needs to go. Canals were first built in Egypt, Mesopotamia, China, and India.

WORDS TO KNOW

Mesopotamia: a region of the Middle East that today is part of Iraq.

flood: when the water in a river or lake overflows.

silt: fine-grained soil rich in nutrients, often found at the bottom of rivers or lakes.

fertile: describes soil that is good for growing crops.

nutrients: substances that living things need to live and grow.

EARLY CANALS IN EGYPT

DID YOU KNOW?

Nearly 60 percent of the world's freshwater is found in fewer than 10 countries—Brazil, Russia, China, Canada, Indonesia, United States, India, Colombia, and the Democratic Republic of Congo.

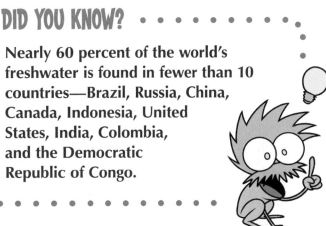

Egypt is one of the driest countries in the world. It receives approximately 2 inches of rain per year. Because there is little rain, Egyptians have always had to rely on the Nile River for their water. Every year, the Nile River floods the farmland around it. The river leaves behind a rich layer of silt that is fertile and full of nutrients.

shaduf: an ancient water-lifting device for irrigation.

WORDS TO KNOW

Around 3000 BCE, Egyptian engineers created an irrigation system to take advantage of the annual flooding. They built flat bottom basins where the water collected whenever the Nile River flooded. These basins were built in a variety of sizes. They could be the size of a pond or a small lake. Gates held the water in the basins.

When the gates were opened, water could move through canals to fill smaller ditches between farmers' fields. Farmers used this water for irrigating crops, such as barley.

Egyptians farmers used a tool called a shaduf to lift water from these ditches to their plots. The shaduf looked like a giant see-saw. At one end was a bucket to carry the water and at the other end was a rock. The shaduf balanced on a frame. When the weight dropped, the bucket was lifted up.

SIMPLE MACHINES

A **simple machine** makes work easier. The screw, inclined plane, **lever**, **pulley**, wedge, and wheel and axle are simple machines. A shaduf is an example of a simple machine. The shaduf's long arm works as a lever. When force is applied to one end of the arm, the load on the other end moves.

simple machine: a tool that uses one movement to complete work.

lever: a bar that rests on a support and lifts or moves things.

pulley: a wheel with a groove for a rope used to lift a load.

watershed: the area of land that drains into a river or a lake.

downstream: farther down a river in the direction a river or stream flows.

WORDS TO KNOW

FROM CANALS TO DAMS

Engineers often build dams to stop flooding in places where there is too much water. What happens when you pour more and more water into a cup? It overflows! Imagine that your cup is a river and the rain is adding water to the river. What happens? A flood! Dams can keep all that extra water from flooding the banks of a river and causing damage to towns and cities that are near the river.

The state of Oklahoma, for example, has more than 2,000 small dams. Most of these were built to control flooding in **watersheds**. The dams trap and store water in their reservoirs after a heavy downpour. This helps to prevent flooding **downstream**.

KNOCK, KNOCK — WHO'S THERE? WATER — WATER WHO? HA HA HA *Water you doing at my house?*

CANALS AND DAMS!

Some dams help with navigation by controlling a river's water level. The Ohio River is one example. The river has 20 dams. These dams make the river deep enough for ships to carry people and goods, such as coal, from Pittsburgh, Pennsylvania, to the Mississippi River. The Mississippi River is one of the most important shipping routes in the world.

Large dams are also built to produce hydroelectric power. The Grand Coulee Dam is the largest hydroelectric facility in the United States. Every year, the dam generates enough energy for 2.3 million homes! You'll learn more about how hydroelectricity works later in this book. Now that you know what canals and dams are used for, let's learn about how they're built!

? CONSIDER AND DISCUSS

It's time to consider and discuss: How are canals and dams connected to the world's water supply?

THE GRAND COULEE DAM

(CREDIT: FARWESTERN/GREGG M. ERICKSON)

Watch a video about the Grand Coulee Dam from 1987. Even then, engineers considered making water reusable. The water used is returned to the river to be used again. Why is this important?

KEYWORD PROMPTS

Grand Coulee Dam video 🔍

PROJECT!

CREATE A SLOGAN

Imagine that you are a real estate agent in the future, when people are living on different planets. You are going to design a slogan that advertises Earth's water to encourage people to move back to Earth. This activity can be done with a partner or team.

1 In your engineering notebook, write down a list of adjectives that describe water. Think about what it looks and feels like and how it moves. Reread the section in this chapter that talks about how much freshwater there is in the world. Write down some of the important facts in your journal.

2 Think about positive ways you can talk about Earth's water. A slogan is a phrase used in advertising that is easy to remember. With permission from an adult, research slogans for companies. This will help you come up with slogan ideas. Write a list of positive statements about Earth's water and choose one slogan for a bumper sticker.

3 Cut a 3-by-11½-inch rectangle from scrap paper for your bumper sticker. Use the pencils or markers to write the slogan and decorate your bumper sticker. Display your sticker when you are done.

TRY THIS! In a group, create a commercial about the importance of water based on your slogan. You can use music and dance to make your commercial memorable.

SUPPLIES

* engineering notebook and pencil
* scrap paper
* colored pencils, markers, and crayons

THEN & NOW

THEN: In 1895, Nikola Tesla (1856–1943) and George Westinghouse (1846–1914) built the world's first hydroelectric power plant over the Niagara Falls in New York.

NOW: Hydropower supplies 16 percent of the world's electricity.

19

CREATE A WATERSHED

Where does water go when it falls as rain? In this activity, you will explore the path of rainwater by building a model of a watershed.

SUPPLIES

* engineering notebook and pencil
* tray, if doing activity inside
* assorted small plastic containers
* large plastic bag
* water bottle

1 Before you begin, start a scientific method worksheet in your notebook and write down a prediction. How much water is needed before a river begins to form in the model? A hypothesis could be: We believe we can empty half a water bottle before a river begins to form.

2 Set up your experiment outside on a flat space. Or, set up your experiment inside on a tray. Place the tray on the floor or other flat surface.

3 Arrange your plastic containers around the area. Leave gaps between the containers.

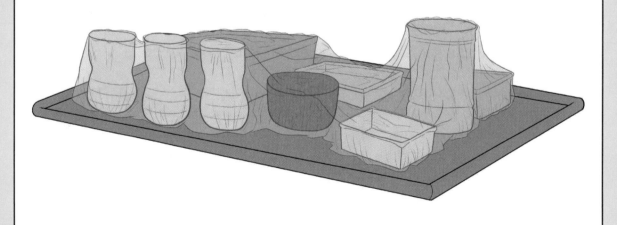

4 Cut along the sides of the plastic bag to make a flat sheet. Place this over the containers. Fold the extra plastic under the containers so water doesn't spill off the tray.

5 Spray water over the plastic sheet. What do you notice happening? Where does the water go? Write down your observations in your engineering notebook.

TRY THIS! What effect would a dam have on your landscape? With permission from an adult, create a huge landscape outdoors with a plastic drop cloth. Use the engineering design process and an engineering design worksheet. Place objects under the sheet and spray with water. Next, put a barrier such as pebbles across one of the rivers on the sheet. Spray again. Did your dam work the way you wanted it to? What changes would you make?

EXPLORE A WATERSHED

Watersheds are areas of land where water collects. Some of the water seeps into the ground and is stored there. This becomes **groundwater**. People tap into this water with wells. Some water does not seep into the ground, but flows over the land as **runoff**. The water flows into rivers, lakes, and oceans.

WORDS TO KNOW

groundwater: water that is underground in spaces between rocks.

runoff: water that flows off the land into bodies of water.

PROJECT!

WATER CYCLE

The water cycle is happening all around you! In this activity, you will study the processes of evaporation and condensation.

1 Place the smaller cereal bowl in the center of the larger bowl on a flat surface.

2 For the land, tear off clumps of clay the size of golf balls. Gently push them into the bottom of the large bowl. Arrange most of the pebbles and shells on the clay.

3 Fill the jug with about 2 cups of water. If you want, add a few drops of blue food coloring. Add the water to the large bowl, but do not fill past the rim of the smaller bowl.

4 Cover the large bowl tightly with plastic wrap. Place a few pebbles on the plastic wrap, directly above the small bowl. Place the bowl in the sun or under a lamp.

5 Start a scientific method worksheet for your observations. What happens to the small bowl? Where does this water come from? How is this similar to the water cycle?

TRY THIS! Before beginning your experiment use a thermometer to check the temperature of your bowl. After the water has condensed, peel back the wrap and check the temperature again.

SUPPLIES

* large mixing bowl
* small cereal bowl
* clay
* 1 cup pebbles, shells
* water
* mixing jug
* blue food coloring (optional)
* mixing spoon
* plastic wrap

MAKE A SHADUF

The shaduf is still used to lift water in some countries. In this activity, you will make a shaduf.

SUPPLIES

* 2 paper towel rolls
* scissors
* 2 empty jars
* 2 strong sticks about 1 foot long
* disposable plastic cup
* string
* bucket

1 Cut out rectangles from one side of the top of each paper towel roll. Place the two jars slightly less than 1 foot apart from one another. Put the paper towel rolls into the jars. Allow one of the sticks to rest in the cuts of your paper towel rolls. This keeps it from rolling away.

2 With the help of an adult, make three holes near the top of your plastic cup. Cut five 4-inch pieces of string. Tie three of these strings to the holes in the cup. Then, tie them together above the cup. Use the fourth piece of string to attach the cup and string to the second stick. Use the fifth piece of string to tie the center of the second stick to the stick on the shaduf stand.

TRY THIS! Fill the bucket with water, and place it in front of and below your shaduf. Try lifting water into a flower pot with your shaduf. Does it work? If not, what can you adjust to make it work? Try adding a weight to the end of your shaduf.

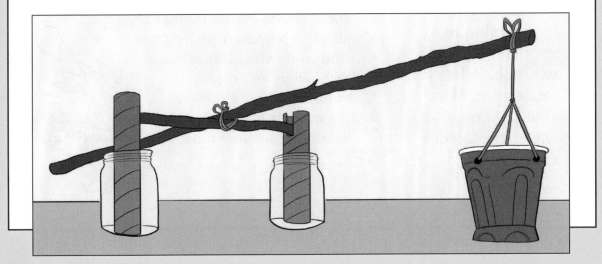

PROJECT!

USE YOUR HANDS AS A DAM

Can your hands work like a dam? In a story from the Netherlands, a tale is told of a little boy who sticks his finger in a crumbling dike to hold back the sea and saves his country. In this activity, you will discover if your hands can stop the flow of water.

1 Start a scientific method worksheet and write down a question. For example, "Will my hands be able to stop the flow of water?"

2 Turn on the cold water tap. Decide whether you will lace your fingers together, cup your hands, or do both. Then, make a dam with your hands.

3 How will you stop the water from going down the drain? Decide where to place your hands to stop the water from escaping.

4 What is happening to the water in the sink? Were you able to stop it from going down the drain?

THINK ABOUT IT:

If you decrease or increase the amount of water flowing out of the tap, how would this affect your experiment? How could you make less water flow through your fingers?

DID YOU KNOW?

Dams provide water for up to 30 to 40 percent of all irrigated land worldwide. This means that billions of people around the world rely on the water from canals and dams to grow their food.

24

PHASE 1
DESIGN
NOMAD DAM
FULL DESIGN
LOCATITION:
SPURLING, WEST
PERMITS OBTAINED
MATERIALS ON
CONTRACTS
PHASE 2
CONSTRUCTION
24 MONTHS
ESTIMATED
PHASE 3
IMPLEMENTATION
POWER
EXPECT
IN THE
6 MONTHS
FULL
POWER
TO 3

CHAPTER 2

ENGINEERING AND DESIGN

What do you do during a brainstorming session? This is when you think of ideas to come up with a solution to a challenge. Engineers use their training and experience to brainstorm solutions to challenges when building dams and canals, because no two dams or canals are exactly alike.

Every building project presents new challenges during construction. A steep canyon, towering mountain, or a series of villages might lie directly in the path of the structure. At the beginning of each project, engineers ask lots of questions. What will the structure be used for? How much water will flow through it? How will it affect the ecosystem?

WORDS TO KNOW

ecosystem: a community of animals and plants existing and interacting together.

CANALS AND DAMS!

? INVESTIGATE!

What structures do dams and canals have in common?

To answer these questions, engineers take samples of rock. They measure the moisture in the soil. They use computers, GPS, and field surveys to map land features.

Engineers also learn about natural hazards common to the area, such as landslides, wildfires, and earthquakes. Even though technology helps predict natural disasters, a canal or dam could still weaken under certain conditions. Engineers try to plan for these events to prevent damage.

The Oroville Dam is the tallest dam in the United States. It stands 770 feet high! The dam spans the Feather River in California. People thought the dam was an engineering achievement, but in 2017, the dam's spillway broke after heavy storms. Thousands of people had to be evacuated from the area and from their homes.

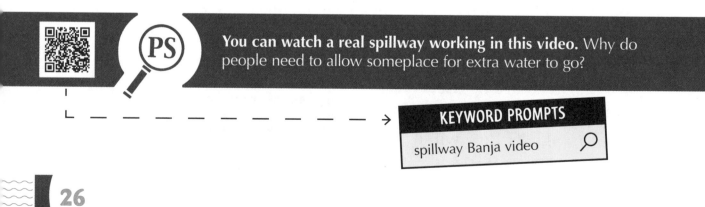

PS **You can watch a real spillway working in this video.** Why do people need to allow someplace for extra water to go?

KEYWORD PROMPTS

spillway Banja video

26

pressure: a force that
pushes on an object.

WORDS ⊙ KNOW

Repair crews fought to fix
the spillway before it gave way
completely. Crews used helicopters
to drop boulders into holes in the spillway. Fortunately, the
storms stopped, and the spillway did not collapse.

DAMS AND FORCES

A dam must be strong to resist forces pushing and pulling on
it. For example, gravity is an invisible force pulling everything
downward. Without it, lakes, rivers, and people would float
into space! If a dam didn't resist gravity, it would collapse.

Water pressure is another strong force that dams must
resist. Have your ears ever hurt when you dove underwater?
That pain is caused by pressure. As you dive deeper, the water
pressure gets stronger because there is more water pressing
down on you.

CAPE COD CHALLENGE

About 25,000 years ago, a glacier moved over what is now Cape Cod
in Massachusetts. It left behind enormous boulders. Some boulders
weighed up to 100 tons! When construction began on the Cape Cod
Canal in 1909, moving these massive rocks became a major engineering
challenge. At that time, these rocks were too heavy for machines to
lift. Engineers hired divers, who risked their lives to plant explosives to
blast the boulders out of the way. People still use the 7-mile-long canal
to travel between Cape Cod Bay north of Cape Cod and Buzzards Bay
south of Cape Cod.

Engineers must design a dam to withstand the pressure of the water. They meet this challenge by making a dam wider at its base. The Shasta Dam in California is one of the tallest dams in the United States. The dam's top is 30 feet wide, but its base is almost 18 times this size. It is 543 feet wide!

DID YOU KNOW?

The Shasta Dam provided much-needed energy to the factories that produced weapons and equipment during World War II. However, it is a controversial structure because of the environmental damage and destruction to Native American tribal lands that it causes.

THE SHASTA DAM BEING BUILT IN 1942. YOU CAN SEE HOW MUCH WIDER THE BASE IS THAN THE TOP.
(CREDIT: RUSSELL LEE)

CONSTRUCTING CANALS

After engineers complete their studies of a building site, the design process begins. Civil engineers use geometric shapes for their canal designs. One popular shape is a trapezoid. A trapezoid makes the slope of the canal walls more stable.

Digging the canal is the next step. The earliest canals were built by hand. Workers used shovels to dig out the earth, saws to cut down trees, and wheelbarrows to take away the dirt. Later, workers used horse-drawn plows.

For example, in 1785, work began on the Patowmack Canal in Virginia. During the next 16 years, slaves and paid workers dug the canal by hand. To make the canal deep enough for shallow boats, workers had to dredge the silt from its bottom. To keep the water from leaking out, they lined the canal bed with clay.

Today, some massive canals are as wide as a football field. Imagine digging a canal that size by hand! Luckily, modern construction workers use heavy machinery to dig the channel instead.

civil engineering: a branch of engineering that deals with designing structures such as dams, canals, tunnels, or bridges.

concrete: a hard material for construction made with cement, sand, and water.

towpath: a path along a canal traveled by horses pulling boats.

legging: people using their feet to push against a tunnel wall to propel a boat.

WORDS TO KNOW

DID YOU KNOW?

There are nearly 200 different types of engineering! The type of engineering that deals with canals and dams is called civil engineering.

After the channel is dug, the walls are firmed up with materials such as concrete. This prevents water from seeping out of the canal.

Tunnels are cut to carry canals through hills and mountains. Before there were engines, horses were used to pull boats along a towpath. How did a boat get through the tunnel? Boat crews had to leg it through tunnels.

Legging required the crew to lie on their backs on each side of the boat. They pressed their feet against the tunnel wall and walked the boat down it! An experienced legger could move a boat about a mile an hour.

diversion tunnel: a tunnel built to redirect a portion of a river.

WORDS TO KNOW

CREATING DAMS

When designing a dam, it isn't possible to pick up a river and set it down somewhere else. So, engineers do the next best thing. They build a long canal called a **diversion tunnel** to temporarily guide the river away from the construction site.

WHAT IS TALLER THAN THE LARGEST DAM ON EARTH?

HA HA HA

A library! It has the most stories.

Teams of construction workers dig the tunnel from both ends. They use massive drilling machines to grind chunks of rock loose. Excavators scoop up the earth and rock with mechanical arms and dump the earth into nearby trucks. Then, the dirt is stored near the dam. It might be used to fill the dam or to build up the slopes of the dam.

Next, workers build cofferdams to keep water and soil out of the building site. The simplest type of cofferdam is built of earth and has a clay core. A larger cofferdam is constructed with wood or double steel walls called sheet piles. After that, the space between the walls is filled with gravel, rock, or sand. When the building site is drained of water, workers dig until they reach the bedrock. This is a solid base on which to build the dam's foundations.

BRIDGES AND TUNNELS

Sometimes, engineers design bridges and tunnels as part of canal projects. Bridges allow pedestrians, cars, and trains to move from one side of a canal to the other. A type of bridge called an aqueduct carries canals across valleys.

THE PONT DU GARD IS A FAMOUS ROMAN AQUEDUCT IN FRANCE.
(CREDIT: MARION SCHNEIDER AND CHRISTOPH AISTLEITNER)

THEN: The first known cofferdam was built in 539 BCE to change the course of the Euphrates River. It was built for King Cyrus of Persia (590–529 BCE), who wanted his armies to capture the city of Babylon in modern-day Iraq.

NOW: Engineers built three cofferdams during the construction of the Three Gorges Dam in China. The last cofferdam was taken down in 2006 with enough explosives to topple 400 10-story buildings!

BUILDING THE HOOVER DAM

The Hoover Dam is one of America's "Seven Modern Civil Engineering Wonders." When construction began in 1931, engineers faced their first challenge. How were they going to move the Colorado River? The river had flowed along its 1,400-mile-long course for millions of years!

Engineers solved this problem by diverting the river through four enormous tunnels. Each tunnel was as wide as a four-lane highway and as deep as a five-story building is high! People worked in teams, 24 hours a day, to carve their way through the rock. This was very slow work.

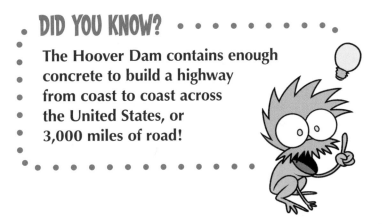

DID YOU KNOW?

The Hoover Dam contains enough concrete to build a highway from coast to coast across the United States, or 3,000 miles of road!

DRILLING JUMBO (CREDIT: DEPARTMENT OF THE INTERIOR)

But engineers had a big idea! They built large trucks called jumbo trucks for the job. Each truck had platforms on the back for up to 30 workers. As the truck backed into the tunnel, workers jackhammered holes into the rock for explosives. One ton of dynamite cleared away 14 feet of rock at a time. The finished tunnels could carry more than 1.5 million gallons of water each second!

Now you know some of the ways engineers plan dams and canals. In the next chapter, we'll take a look at what makes these structures strong enough to withstand the forces around them!

? CONSIDER AND DISCUSS

It's time to consider and discuss: What structures do dams and canals have in common?

PROJECT!

QUENCH YOUR THIRST

Roman engineers built aqueducts all over the Mediterranean region. Imagine that you have been hired as a Roman water engineer.

1 Your challenge is to build an aqueduct from a mountain spring (your bucket) to different sites in your city. Start an engineering design worksheet and brainstorm plans to deliver water to the city.

2 Through trial and error, set up a course with the cereal boxes and plastic containers. Then, use the duct tape to secure the tubing or the straws to each building. Be sure to have the tube empty into a container at the end of the course!

> **DID YOU KNOW?**
>
> **The Romans often lined their aqueducts with a material called pozzolana, which was made from volcanic ash!**

3 Lower your tube into the water in the bucket and then raise the tube so the water starts to flow toward the city. What happens? Record your observations in your journal.

4 Can you improve the flow of water? Can you make it move more quickly or slowly? Change the course and write down your design changes in your notebook. Does your system work better? What can you do to improve it further?

TRY THIS! Set a time challenge. Can you deliver water to your city faster? Why is this important for cities?

SUPPLIES

* engineering notebook and pencil
* empty cereal boxes, plastic containers, and other small obstacles
* clear tubing or flexible straws joined together with tape
* duct tape
* bucket of water
* empty container

PROJECT!

UNDER PRESSURE

In this experiment, we'll investigate water pressure. Why do engineers make the wall of a dam wider at the bottom than the top?

SUPPLIES

* water bottle
* pushpin
* masking tape
* engineering notebook and pencil

1 Use the pushpin to make three holes in the side of the water bottle at different heights. Place a strip of masking tape over the holes. Place the bottle in a sink and fill it with water.

2 Write a prediction in your journal. When you rip off the tape, which stream of water will travel the furthest?

3 Rip off the tape. How does the water flow out of each hole? Why? Write down your observations and conclusions in your notebook. Use a bar graph to track your results.

THINK MORE: Think about water pressure in a reservoir. Where would this pressure be the lowest and where would it be the greatest? Why?

PRESSURE POP!

Have you ever dived into a pool or lake and felt your ears pop? You're feeling the effects of water pressure! When you are near the surface of the water, you don't feel any different because the fluids in your body are pushing out against the pressure of the water around you. But when you dive deeper, there's more water pressure pushing on your body, and you can feel it in your ears.

PROJECT!

WATERTIGHT!

Cofferdams are used to keep a work site dry. In this engineering challenge, how will you make your cofferdam watertight?

SUPPLIES

* engineering notebook and pencil
* foil pie plate or takeout container
* sand
* water
* disposable cup
* scissors
* turkey baster

1 Start an engineering design worksheet and, brainstorm designs for a watertight cofferdam. How will you keep the water contained? What materials do you need?

2 Pour sand into the bottom of the pie plate until it is about 1 to 2 inches deep. Pour water on top of the sand until it is covered.

3 Use the scissors to cut the top and bottom off the disposable cup. Push it into the sand and water. The cup represents the inner wall of the cofferdam.

4 Make sure the water level is even inside and outside of the cup. Next, use the turkey baster to empty the water from inside the cup. How watertight is your cofferdam? Record your results in your notebook.

THINK MORE: What was the most challenging problem you had? What would you change about your design? Test your idea.

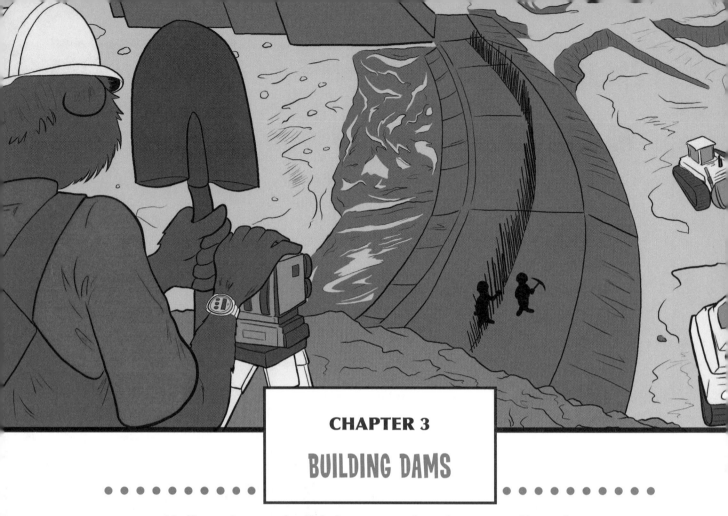

CHAPTER 3

BUILDING DAMS

Civil engineers build dams ranging from small 10-foot-wide farm structures to dams so large that cars can drive across them. Some projects become famous. For example, the Itaipu Dam is one of the largest hydroelectric dams in the world. In 1996, the American Society of Civil Engineers and *Popular Mechanics* magazine declared the dam one of the seven wonders of the modern world!

While there are many thousands of dams in the world, civil engineers design and build four basic types. These are gravity, arch, buttress, and embankment dams.

? **INVESTIGATE!**

What shapes are used to give dams strength?

GRAVITY DAMS

The gravity dam gets its name from the way its bulky size keeps it from moving. When water pushes against the dam's wall, the weight of the dam holds it in place. Gravity dams are built with concrete. Because concrete is so heavy, engineers choose a site with solid rock to keep the dam stable.

Gravity dams are often built in wide valleys to prevent flooding. Their other jobs include producing hydroelectric power and improving navigation.

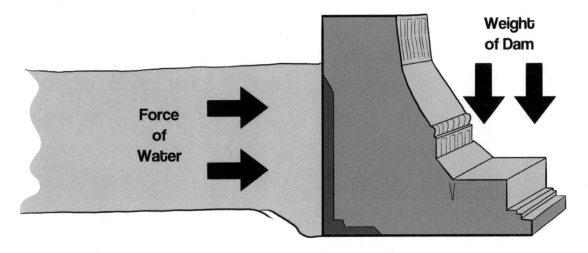

Engineers have been building gravity dams for thousands of years. One of the earliest gravity dams was built in Mesopotamia around 3000 BCE. It is called the Jawa Dam. The dam had two stone walls and a core filled with crushed stone. Ancient engineers designed the dam to provide water for irrigation.

CANALS AND DAMS!

ARCH DAMS

The arch dam is the thinnest type of dam built today. Engineers usually build this style of dam in canyons where the steep walls help support the dam. The arch dam looks like a giant letter C. The reservoir is on the outer, or convex, side. When water pushes against the curve, the arch sends the force to either side. The sides of the dam press against the walls of the canyon, which push back and keep the dam in place.

THE HOOVER DAM IS BOTH AN ARCH DAM AND A GRAVITY DAM

Archimedes screw: a device with a spiral used to raise water.

WORDS ⓣⓞ KNOW

In the first century BCE, Roman engineers built the earliest known arch dam in Vallon de Baume, France. It is called the Glanum Dam. The Romans wanted the dam so they could supply a nearby town with water. Workers moved large stone blocks into place with simple machines, such as pulleys and inclined planes, called ramps, to build the 39-foot-high dam.

ROMAN ENGINEERING

Roman engineers used simple machines, including pulleys and levers, to build dams. One machine, called a pile driver, pushed columns into the ground. The columns supported a dam while it was being built. The pile driver was made of wood. It used a pulley with a heavy stone attached to it. When workers released the stone, it dropped onto the column, driving it into the ground.

Another machine used to build dams was the **Archimedes screw.** This was a hollow pipe with a long spiral inside of it. This machine was invented by Archimedes (287–212 BCE), a Greek mathematician and a great problem-solver. Roman workers placed one end of the screw into water. As they turned the screw, the building site was drained as water traveled upward.

 (PS) **You can watch an Archimedes screw in action in this video.** How does the water defeat gravity?

KEYWORD PROMPTS
Archimedes screw video 🔍

BUTTRESS DAMS

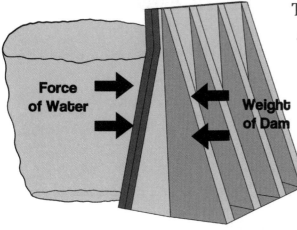

Force of Water

Weight of Dam

The buttress dam is built with a series of triangular-shaped structures called buttresses. When water pushes on the dam, the buttresses along the side that faces downstream support the dam and keep it from toppling over. This style of dam is built with concrete and reinforced steel in areas with wide river valleys.

Some buttress dams are built with arches. The Daniel-Johnson Dam in Quebec, Canada, is the highest multiple-arch dam in the world! It was built in the 1960s when Quebec needed more energy. Three thousand workers spent seven years building the massive dam. The amount of concrete used in the dam is enough to build a sidewalk from the North Pole to the South Pole!

DID YOU KNOW?

The Monticello Dam in California has a spillway shaped like a bathtub drain. This type of spillway is called a morning glory. The Monticello Dam's morning glory is the largest in the world. In just one second, it can drain an Olympic-sized swimming pool is worth of water!

PS You can see a video of the Monticello Dam's spillway in action at this website.

KEYWORD PROMPTS

WaPo morning glory

erosion: the gradual wearing away of rock or soil by water and wind.

riprap: chunks of stone used to prevent erosion.

WORDS TO KNOW

EMBANKMENT DAMS

The embankment dam is the most popular type of dam built today. It looks like a small mountain with layers of earth, sand, soil, and rock. Engineers bring in machines with heavy rollers to flatten each layer. The dam's slopes must be protected from water damage and erosion with loose stone called riprap. The riprap prevents water from leaking through the earth and rock.

The Mica Dam is one of the largest earth-filled dams in the world. It stands 797 feet tall and is located on the Columbia River in Canada. The dam can produce enough hydroelectric power for more than 650,000 homes!

THE MICA DAM

PARTS OF A DAM

A dam typically includes a foundation, cutoff wall, main wall, spillway, and reservoir. The foundation is the material on which the dam is built, such as bedrock. It must support the weight of the dam. The cutoff wall is a type of watertight ditch. It prevents water from seeping beneath the foundation. A dam's main wall might be built with concrete, soil, or rock. The spillway carries water away from a dam. It usually looks like a long narrow chute. The reservoir is an artificial lake that holds the water blocked by the dam. All these parts of a dam work together.

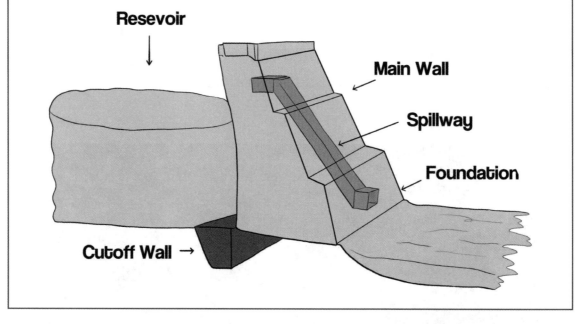

NATURAL DAMS

Not all dams are made by people to make a place better to live. Landslides can create natural dams. A landslide is a powerful natural disaster. A heavy rainstorm, melting snow, or an earthquake can lead to a landslide.

Hills can weaken when they can't absorb all that moisture. Rocks and mud begin to slide, and pick up everything in their path. A landslide can move as fast as 30 feet per second! Trees, cars, and homes can be swept up in the slide. Some landslides can block a valley. They may also dam streams or rivers.

In 2015, a strong earthquake struck Nepal. It triggered a huge and deadly landslide. Ice and car-sized boulders from one of the highest peaks in Nepal, Mount Langtang, began hurtling downward. The landslide buried the village below it. The rocks, sand, and ice blocked the Langtang River, creating a natural dam.

Now that you've learned how dams are built, we'll take a look at canals. Are the same shapes used to create strong canals that can hold lots of water? Let's find out!

? CONSIDER AND DISCUSS

It's time to consider and discuss: What shapes are used to give dams strength?

EXPLORE EARTHEN DAMS

The most common type of dam is an earthen dam. In this experiment, you will see how strong earthen dams are.

1 Which material will best hold back water? Gravel, sand, or soil? Start a scientific method worksheet and write a prediction in your engineering notebook. Create a chart like the one show here to record what you see.

	Prediction	Result
Gravel		
Sand		
Soil		

2 Pour the gravel into the center of the pan. Mold the gravel with your hands to make an earthen dam across the entire pan.

3 Slowly pour water behind the dam. Note how much water you pour so you can pour the same amount in steps 6 and 7.

PROJECT!

4 Use your timer to see how long it takes for the water to escape to the other side of the dam. Record your results in your engineering notebook.

5 Empty the water out of your pan. Place the gravel to one side. You will be using it again.

6 Repeat steps 2 to 5 with the sand. Repeat steps 2 to 5 with the soil.

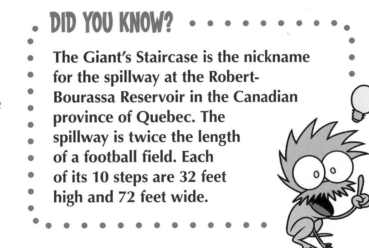

DID YOU KNOW?

The Giant's Staircase is the nickname for the spillway at the Robert-Bourassa Reservoir in the Canadian province of Quebec. The spillway is twice the length of a football field. Each of its 10 steps are 32 feet high and 72 feet wide.

7 Now, build an earthen dam with all three materials. Pour water behind the dam. Write down your observations in your engineering notebook. Compare your prediction with your data.

THINK ABOUT IT: Gravel, sand, and soil have different-sized grains. The size of the grain affects how fast water passes through the material. Do larger or smaller grains allow more water to pass through?

TRY THIS! Instead of soil, use silt. Silt can be collected from a nearby stream with an adult. Repeat the experiment with silt and compare your results.

SUPPLIES

* engineering notebook and pencil
* large marshmallows
* sour candy belts
* scissors
* pennies

WHICH IS THE STRONGEST?

Civil engineers use strong shapes to make canals and dams stable. In this experiment, you will test a beam and an arch.

1 Which do you think is stronger? A beam or an arch? Start a scientific method worksheet and make a prediction.

2 Put a sour candy belt across two marshmallows. How far apart should you space the marshmallows? How long should you make the belt? Use trial and error to find the best lengths.

3 How much weight can the sour candy beam support? Add one penny at a time to the center of the candy. Record your results in your engineering notebook. How does your data compare with your prediction?

4 Remove the pennies. Gently bend a second piece of candy into an arch and place it beneath the first.

5 Add one penny at a time to the center of the candy. Record your results in your notebook and compare your data with your prediction. Which shape is stronger?

THINK ABOUT IT: Why do engineers use arches in their structures? Can you find examples of arches in other things around you?

TRY THIS! Do you think your results will be different if the beam and arch are shorter or longer? Conduct this experiment again and compare your results.

WORDS TO KNOW

beam: a strong horizontal structure that provides support.

TRIANGLES AND STABILITY

Engineers use triangles to build dams. Triangles help to create stability. When a buttress is attached to a dam wall, it forms a triangle. Are triangles stronger than a beam?

1 Start a scientific method worksheet in your engineering notebook and write a prediction. Put a piece of paper across two yogurt containers. Add one penny at a time to the middle of the paper. You can cut the paper to make it stronger. Record your results.

2 Now, fold the paper back and forth to make an accordion. Place the paper on top of the yogurt containers.

3 Add pennies, one at a time, to the paper. Record your results and compare them with your prediction.

THINK ABOUT IT: What type of force does a buttress experience? Investigate buildings near you. How do these structures use triangles?

THEN & NOW

THEN: Early dam engineers did not consider how dams blocked or slowed down fish migration.

NOW: Engineers build fish ladders to help fish get around dams. The ladders are a series of pools. The fish leap from pool to pool until they have passed the dam.

WORDS TO KNOW

fish ladder: a series of pools that allow fish to swim around a dam.

PROJECT!

TALL AND THIN

How will you design and build an arch dam that holds back water? Building your dam will mean trying out new things.

1 Place the loaf pan on a flat surface. Use some of the clay, sand, mud, and pebbles to form a narrow **gorge** down the sides of the pan. Decide how much you need of each item.

2 Use the plastic knife to make a notch in the middle of both sides of the gorge. These notches are for the ends of your arch dam.

3 Pick up the remaining clay and mold it with your hands into an arch. Arch dams are thin and curved. The bottom and sides of an arch dam are thicker than the top. When you are pleased with your dam, fit it into the notches on each side. The notches will help support your dam.

4 If your dam begins to slide, remove it. Roll it back into a ball and cover it with plastic wrap so that it does not dry out. Start an engineering design worksheet and brainstorm possible ways that you can solve this problem. For example, what will happen if you make the base wider?

SUPPLIES

* loaf pan
* air-dry clay
* sand, mud, and pebbles
* plastic knife
* jug of water
* engineering notebook and pencil

WORDS TO KNOW

gorge: a deep, narrow passage.

5 Make a new dam and attach it. Slowly pour water behind the arch, into the reservoir. What happens?

6 Record the results in your journal and compare your prediction with your data.

TRY THIS! Do you think your results would be different if you let your dam harden? Allow the dam to rest for a few hours. Try this experiment again. Next, allow the dam to harden overnight. Test your dam and compare your results.

ICE DAMS

Ice dams form in rivers when chunks of melting ice collide downstream. In extremely cold regions, when ice sheets and glaciers move, they can form dams, too. One glacier in Alaska is frequently on the move. It's called the Hubbard Glacier and is 76 miles long! In 1986, the glacier's ice dam turned a thin strip of water called the Russell Fjord near the Alaskan coast into a lake for several months.

PS Visit this NASA site to see how the Hubbard Glacier advanced.

KEYWORD PROMPTS

NASA Hubbard Glacier advance 🔍

PROJECT!

AMAZING ARCHIMEDES

In this activity, you will build an Archimedes screw and investigate ways to use it.

1 Twist the plastic tubing around the outside of the cylinder. Use pieces of duct tape to hold the tube in place. Put to one side.

2 Fill one mixing bowl half full with water. Add a drop of food coloring. Place the second mixing bowl beside the first.

3 Now, place one end of the cylinder in the bowl of colored water. Twist the cylinder as you move it around the bowl to lift the water.

4 Write down what you see in your notebook.

THINK ABOUT IT: Ask an adult to help you investigate how the Archimedes screw is used today in industries such as mining and agriculture. You can do research online and at the library. Where can you find Archimedes screws today?

WHAT DIDN'T ROMANS USE TO BUILD AQUEDUCTS AND CANALS?

HA HA HA

A big pair of Caesars!

EXPERIMENT WITH GLACIERS

How do glaciers melt and move? Find out by making a model!

1 With the marker, label the containers 1 to 3. To make your glaciers, fill each container about a quarter full with sand, pebbles, and water. Use different amounts of sand, pebbles, and water in each container. In your engineering notebook, describe how much you used for each.

2 Place the containers in the freezer. When they have frozen, repeat step 1 until you have filled the containers. The last layer in each container must be water. Place the containers back in the freezer.

3 Take one of the frozen containers out of the freezer. Warm the sides of the container under warm water to help release the glacier.

4 Prop up one end of a baking sheet on the book or something similar. Place the glacier at the top of the baking sheet. For the next hour or so, write down what you see in your notebook. Repeat this step with the other containers.

TRY THIS! Attach a string around the middle of one of the glaciers and tape the string to the top edge of the baking sheet. How are your results the same or different?

THINK ABOUT IT: Look at the debris your glaciers created. Think about how the debris from an actual glacier shapes the land. How does this help you understand how a glacier can form a dam?

WORDS TO KNOW

debris: the remains of something, such as dirt, rocks, and vegetation.

CHAPTER 4

COOL CANALS

· ·

What happens if you are building a canal and come across obstacles such as hills and valleys? You can't flatten the landscape in order to keep the water in the canal at one level, right?

· ·

This was a challenge for ancient civil engineers. One solution thought of by inventive engineers was to create direct routes using tunnels and aqueducts. Later, engineers built  locks to carry ships up and down hills. Canal locks are like huge steps. Their job is to move ships between different water levels.

? **INVESTIGATE!**

How do locks improve trade and navigation?

More than 2,000 years ago, engineers in China created the first locks, called flash locks. Flash locks were simple wooden gates across a canal. Workers raised or lowered the gates with a rope wrapped around a type of pulley called a windlass.

When a boat was going downstream, the surge of water quickly pushed the boat through the passage. But when the boat was going upstream, workers had to pull it against the current.

lock: an engineering feature on canals that helps raise or lower boats from one level of water to another.

windlass: a device that uses a rope wound around a barrel to raise objects.

upstream: the direction opposite to the flow of a stream or river.

current: the steady flow of water in one direction.

WORDS TO KNOW

CANALS AND DAMS!

capstan: an upright cylinder that turns to wind a rope or cable.

WORDS TO KNOW

Canals in ancient China were often built on flat land to avoid hills. When there was a hill, workers hauled the boat over a ramp called a slipway with ropes attached to two capstans.

A capstan looked like a giant wooden spool with bars poking out of the sides. Workers used their muscles to push against the bars. As the capstan turned, the rope wound clockwise and pulled the boat up. When the capstan was turned the other way, the boat would slide down the slipway into another section of the canal.

This system worked, but it was not perfect. Slipways damaged the bottom of the barges. Robbers often stole the goods off the decks!

AN EARLY CANAL LOCK IN CHINA.

(CREDIT: WILLIAM ALEXANDER)

!!!!!

POUND LOCK

Jiao Wei-ye was a Chinese government official and engineer. In 983 CE, he invented the first pound lock. A pound lock had vertical rising gates at the two ends of the lock. After a boat entered the lock, the gate was closed. Water would fill the lock to raise the boat or be drained to lower the boat.

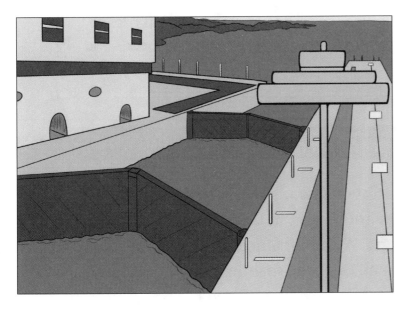

Pound locks solved the problem of boats being damaged or robbed on slipways. These locks were first used on a waterway in China called the Grand Canal.

About 500 years later, in 1458, the first canal in Europe to use pound locks was completed. This canal was called the Bereguardo Canal, in Italy. In that same century, the famous artist and scientist Leonard da Vinci (1452–1519) redesigned the Naviglio Grande with pound locks that used miter gates. Miter gates look like a V when closed, with the V pointing upstream. The pressure of the water keeps the gates tightly closed.

WORDS TO KNOW

valve: a structure that controls the passage of fluid.

Colonial America: the name given to America during the years 1607–1776, when new settlers came from Europe and before the United States became its own country.

trade: the exchange of goods for other goods or money.

HOW LOCKS WORK

A ship enters the lock chamber and the gates close behind it. To lower the ship, the filling **valve** closes and the draining valve opens. The water drains out of the lock until it reaches the downstream level. The downstream gate opens and the ship moves out of the lock and is on its way.

For a ship going upstream, the steps reverse. Once the ship is in the lock, the draining valve closes. Water pours in through the filling valve and the ship rises to the same level as the water upstream. Then, the upstream gate opens and the ship leaves.

THE ERIE CANAL

In the 1700s, it was easier to move goods by water than by road. Roads did not connect every town, and in Colonial America, dirt roads were rough and bumpy. When it rained, the roads became rivers of mud. Leaders such as George Washington (1732–1799) thought that canals would improve communication, trade, and transportation among towns and cities.

The construction of the Erie Canal, the greatest canal building project in the United States, began in the nineteenth century. A politician named DeWitt Clinton (1769–1828) first suggested building the Erie Canal in 1808. He thought a canal linking the Great Lakes with the Hudson River would be good for trade.

immigrant: a person who comes to settle in a new country.

WORDS ⊤O KNOW

Ships could use the canal to haul raw materials such as lumber, apples, and potatoes from the West to markets in the East. Eastern manufacturers could use the canal to sell their goods, including tools and furniture, to settlers heading West. Also, the canal would make it easier for people, including new immigrants, to move across the country.

WHY WAS THE CANAL ANGRY WITH THE BARGE.
HA HA HA
It was always barging in!

The state hired thousands of workers. Teams of horses and mules pulled plows and carts to take away heaps of soil. Workers used gunpowder to blast away walls of sheer rock. On October 26, 1825, the Erie Canal opened. It was 363 miles long!

ERIE CANAL AT LOCKPORT, NEW YORK, AROUND 1855   (CREDIT: PUBLISHED FOR HERRMANN J. MEYER)

A parade of steamboats and canal barges decked out in flags and banners left Albany, New York, for New York City. Men, women, and children crammed the shoreline. They were eager to celebrate this great engineering accomplishment.

The finished canal had 83 locks with miter gates at the front and back that rotated on posts. To open or close a gate, the lock operator pushed on a long beam attached to each side of the gate. Barges were tugged up and down the canal by mules that traveled along towpaths beside the canal. Now, these towpaths make great walking trails!

The canal has been changed and updated since it was first built. Today, it is mostly used for sightseeing cruises, kayaking, and other pleasure boating. Cargo is transported occasionally.

DID YOU KNOW?

The shortest way to travel by sea from Europe to Asia is through the Suez Canal in Egypt. The canal links the Red Sea to the Mediterranean Sea. It allows ships to avoid traveling around the tip of Africa, saving them 6,000 miles.

WATER HIGHWAYS

Canals can also work like water highways within cities. Venice, Italy, is home to a famous canal system. The city is made up of 118 different islands separated by more than 170 canals! The Grand Canal is the largest at 2 miles long. It flows through the city like a giant letter S. Tourist gondolas, water taxis, and barges travel up and down the canal each day.

THE GRAND CANAL IN VENICE, ITALY

(CREDIT: IMAGE COURTESY © 2017 DIGITALGLOBE)

The city of Amsterdam in the Netherlands is also known for its system of canals. Up until the seventeenth century, Amsterdam was mostly marshy land. Then, wealthy citizens began investing in canals to help the city grow. People still use the 165 canals that crisscross the city. They are a popular tourist destination with many small boats slowly moving through the water.

In the next chapter, we'll learn about more famous canals and dams and discover how they've changed the lives of the people who live near them. Some have even changed the entire world!

? CONSIDER AND DISCUSS

It's time to consider and discuss: How do locks improve trade and navigation?

LOCK IT UP OR DOWN

In this activity, you are going to make a model of a lock. You will experiment with filling and emptying the lock to move a ship up or down the container.

1 From the foam sheets, make two gates. The gates need to be the same width as the container to fit tightly.

2 Gently push the gates into the container to divide it into three equal sections.

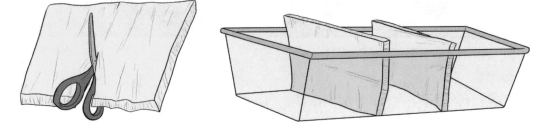

3 Pour the same amount of water into the first two sections. The water level for these sections should be near the top of the container.

4 Pour some water into the third section until it is less than halfway up the container.

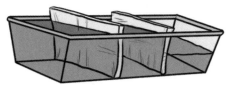

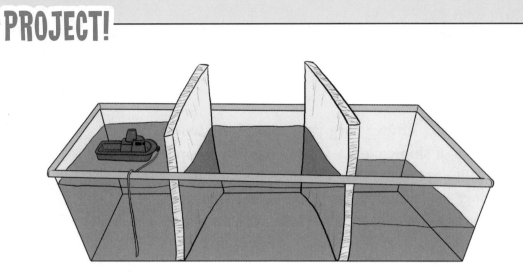

5 Tie a piece of string to the toy boat. Then, place the boat in the first section. Allow the string to drape over the container. Remove the gate between the first and second sections. Guide the boat with the string into the next section and replace the gate behind it.

6 Use the measuring cup to remove water from the second section until the water level is the same as in the third section. Remove the gate between the second and third section. Guide the ship into the last section.

TRY THIS! How can you move the ship upstream? Solve the challenge using your lock!

THEN & NOW

THEN: The first canal locks were made of wood and worked by hand.

- -

NOW: Canal locks are usually made of concrete and reinforced with steel. Many are still operated by hand.

BUILDING BARGES

Container ships move cargo all around the world. One class of ship called a Triple E can carry up to 18,000 containers—that's enough space to transport 111 million pairs of sneakers! How do ships such as these stay afloat? By designing and testing a barge to carry a load, you will discover why ships float.

SUPPLIES

* engineering notebook and pencil
* small plastic container
* aluminum foil
* pennies
* sink and water
* egg carton, popsicle sticks, straws, corks

1 What do you think will happen when you place the plastic container, strip of foil, and penny in water? Start a scientific method worksheet and write down three separate predictions in your engineering notebook.

2 Fill a sink with water. Next, test your predictions. Place one object at a time in the water. Write down what you see.

3 Start an engineering design worksheet and, based on what you saw, build two different types of ships using materials on the supplies list. Your goal is to build a barge that can carry 10 pennies. What material and shape will you choose for your barges? Why?

4 Test one barge at a time. Record the results in your engineering notebook. Is there one material that floats better than others? Why?

TRY THIS! If the barge does not float, think about how you can change the design. Can you build a barge that will hold 10, 15, or 20 pennies?

THINK ABOUT IT: Air fills the space within actual ships. They float because they weigh less than the equal **volume** of water.

WORDS TO KNOW

volume: the amount of space an object takes up.

PROJECT!

A WINDLASS IN ACTION

The ancient Chinese used a windlass to open and close gates on locks. In this project, you will discover how this works.

1 Using the scissors, cut out one side of the milk or juice container. Near the top seam of the container, poke a hole on each side with the scissors. Insert the pencil into these holes.

2 Tie a piece of string to the middle of the pencil. Set the container to one side.

3 Push the wire through the yogurt container and twist to form a handle.

4 Tie the free end of the string to the handle of the yogurt container.

5 How will you wind the thread? Should you twist the pencil away from you or toward you? Write down your prediction in your engineering notebook. Test your prediction. What happens?

THINK ABOUT IT: What are some other uses for a windlass on a dam or canal? How about on a bridge or a skyscraper?

SUPPLIES

* empty half-gallon milk or juice container
* scissors
* pencil
* string
* wire
* small yogurt container or similar container
* engineering notebook and pencil

ENGINEERING CHALLENGE

Create a board game with the goal of building a dam or canal. Engineers use a series of steps to design and problem solve. You will need to come up with problems and solutions to move around the board.

1 In your engineering notebook, write down a theme for your game. Will you be building a canal or a dam? Where is the structure going to be built? Why is it going to be built?

2 Write down four problems and four solutions. For example, spillway fails, workers go on strike, fish cannot migrate. Write down four instructions to get players moving on the board. Don't forget start and finish cards!

3 Cut the colored paper into squares and write your sentences on them with the marker. Arrange the squares around the poster board.

4 Cut out more squares and write more instructions for your game, including skip a turn, free space, move ahead one space, move back one space, roll again, start, and finish. You can also make more challenge cards to add.

5 Once all your cards are written and arranged on the poster board, glue them in place. Add more details to your board with the crayons or with cut-out images from magazines.

6 Play the game with two or more players. Begin by placing your buttons on the start square. The highest roller goes first. The player who reaches the finish first wins the game!

CHAPTER 5

FAMOUS CANALS AND DAMS

Canals and dams have been important to people for thousands of years! They have helped shaped the world into what it is today. The enormous size of these structures and the difficulty in building these projects challenged civil engineers and transformed the land.

Canals and dams have changed the lives of people near them. Let's take a look at a few of the most famous canals and dams in the world.

?

INVESTIGATE!

How are the dams and canals being built today different from those built in the past?

CANALS AND DAMS!

ASWAN HIGH DAM

LOCATION: Aswan, Egypt

TYPE OF DAM: Embankment

Every year between June and September, the Nile River in Egypt used to flood. A huge amount of water was released into the surrounding plains and farmland. Some years, the flood left rich deposits of silt that fertilized the land. Other years, the flooding was so severe that it washed away homes, roads, and buildings in the lands bordering the Nile.

Some years, the river didn't flood enough. When this happened, people couldn't grow enough food to feed everyone. They faced famine.

Starting in 1843, the Egyptians began to create a series of dams to manage the floodwaters and improve irrigation in the region. In 1902, the Egyptians completed the first Aswan Dam. This large buttress dam was built south of the city of Cairo. It was a great engineering triumph. However, as the population grew, the needs of the people became larger than what the dam could provide.

In the 1960s, work began on a new Aswan Dam. Tens of thousands of people had to be moved from the floodpath to new homes. Even though the government also moved thousands of valuable objects, many historical sites could not be saved. The Aswan High Dam took an international team of engineers 10 years to complete. It opened on July 21, 1970.

The Aswan High Dam is more than 2 miles long. About 15 percent of Egypt's electricity is produced by the dam each year. The reservoir also supports a fishing industry. While the dam has helped some people, it has also caused serious problems. The fertilizing silt from the Nile is no longer deposited on nearby farmland because the dam traps the silt behind it. Now, farmers must use artificial fertilizers, which pollute the river.

NILOMETER

The ancient Egyptians built an instrument called a nilometer to measure the water level of the Nile River. A nilometer was a stone column with measurements notched along one side. A low measurement meant that the Nile was not high enough to flood the land. This could mean famine. If the measurement was high, there was a risk of flooding. Why is it important to know flood conditions as early as possible? What kind of instruments do we use today to predict flooding and weather?

(CREDIT: DAVID ROBERTS)

CANALS AND DAMS!

dynasty: a powerful family or group that rules for many years.

peasant: a farmer who lived on and farmed land owned by his lord.

WORDS ᴛᴏ KNOW

CHINA'S GRAND CANAL

LOCATION: Beijing to Hangzhou in China

At 1,100 miles long, the Grand Canal is the longest canal in the world. The northernmost point of the canal is Beijing, the capital of China. The southernmost point is Hangzhou in southern China.

Construction began on the oldest sections of the canal during the Sui dynasty (581–618 BCE). The Grand Canal was built to transport grain from southern China to feed large cities in the north, as well as to move armies in northern China. The northern border was often under attack. Troops and supplies needed to reach this region quickly.

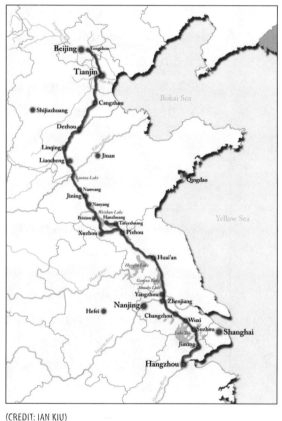

(CREDIT: IAN KIU)

Emperors forced millions of peasants to dig the canal. Workers used simple hand tools, such as pickaxes, to cut through forests, meadows, and wetlands. In some places, workers hand dug the canal a mile wide! They heaved the dirt and rocks away in baskets balanced on long poles over their shoulders. Today, sections of the Grand Canal are still used frequently to transport goods such as construction materials.

THE PANAMA CANAL

LOCATION: Isthmus of Panama

The Panama Canal, completed in 1914, connects the Atlantic and Pacific Oceans through Gatun Lake, the Culebra Cut, and Alajuela Lake. The canal changed sea trade and travel. Before the Panama Canal was built, it could take ships up to five months to sail from New York to San Francisco. They had to sail all the way around South America, which could be a dangerous journey.

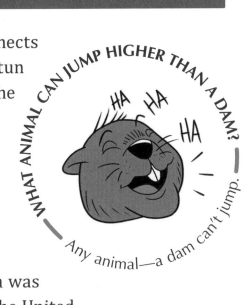

WHAT ANIMAL CAN JUMP HIGHER THAN A DAM?

Any animal—a dam can't jump.

Canal work across the isthmus of Panama was first begun by France. In the early 1900s, the United States took over the building of the canal. Before digging even started, workers had to clear huge areas of jungle. One in three people died from tropical diseases there.

(CREDIT: U.S. NAVY)

penstock: a pipe that leads to a turbine.

turbine: a machine with blades turned by the force of water, air, or steam.

WORDS TO KNOW

Workers faced many more challenges. One of the greatest obstacles was the Culebra Cut. The cut was a treacherous eight-mile section of the canal built through the mountains of Panama. Workers regularly battled landslides, which sometimes trapped them and their machines.

U.S. Army engineer Lieutenant Colonel David du Bose Gaillard (1859–1913) oversaw the Culebra project. His crew of 6,000 men used large steam shovels and explosives to blast through the

DID YOU KNOW?

A fifth of the world's electricity comes from water. China produces the most hydropower in the world. It is followed by Brazil, Canada, the United States, and Russia.

rock. They removed tens of millions of cubic yards of soil. Gaillard died before the end of the project, but his work was recognized by President Woodrow Wilson (1856–1924).

A HYDROELECTRIC POWER PLANT

Hydroelectric power plants consist of a few basic parts. Water from the reservoir flows down a large pipe called a **penstock**. As the water rushes down the penstock, it spins the blades of the **turbines**. A shaft connects the turbines to the generator. The surface of the generator has electromagnets that create electric power as they turn. The electricity from the plant travels on cables to offices, industries, and your home.

shiplift: a platform that is used to lift ships out of the water, move them to a different location, and put them back in the water.

WORDS ⊕ KNOW

The canal finally opened to ships in 1914. The Panama Canal celebrated its 100th birthday in 2014, as engineers were extending and widening the canal to make room for more, larger ships.

THREE GORGES DAM

LOCATION: Hubei, China

TYPE OF DAM: Concrete gravity dam

The Three Gorges Dam was finished in 2009 and is the most powerful hydroelectric dam in the world. The dam spans the Yangtze River in China, the longest river in Asia.

(CREDIT: LE GRAND PORTAGE)

Before the dam was built, China used up to 50 billion tons of coal each year. Now, the dam's 32 generators produce 4 percent of China's total energy needs. The dam has also prevented flooding downstream and improved navigation on the river.

Ships can sail on the Yangtze River from the port of Shanghai to important industrial centers inland. It once took ships up to four hours to travel through the canal's locks. In 2016, civil engineers built the biggest shiplift in the world to speed up the crossing time. Now, the concrete and steel lift moves ships in only 40 minutes.

CANALS AND DAMS!

WORDS ⊚ KNOW

species: a group of plants or animals that are related and look like each other.

extinct: when a species dies out and there are no more left in the world.

Some people think that the dam should not have been built. The dam's reservoir flooded more than a thousand towns and villages, as well as ancient sites.

The dam also destroyed the habitat of rare species, including the Chinese river dolphin, the baiji. In 2006, the dolphin became extinct.

FUTURE STRUCTURES

Canals and dams do have their problems. When a new canal is built, land is destroyed. In Nicaragua, for example, there is a plan to build a canal linking the Pacific Ocean with the Caribbean. If built, rainforests and wetlands would be gone forever. It would destroy the habitat of plants and animals. The canal would also force people out of their homes.

In the Democratic Republic of Congo (DRC), there is a plan to build a new dam on the Congo River. The project is known as the Grand Inga. It would be the largest hydroelectric power project in the world. But the dam would destroy farmland and force thousands of people out of the area.

Today, scientists are studying how people can balance their water needs and care for the environment. Maybe you will be part of the team that comes up with a solution to this challenge!

? CONSIDER AND DISCUSS

It's time to consider and discuss: How are the dams and canals being built today different from those built in the past?

PROJECT!

BUILD AN ARCH

The tallest arch dam in the world is the Jinping-1 Dam in China. It is more than 1,000 feet high. Can you build an arch that will stand up, using only crackers and peanut butter?

1 Which part of an arch needs support? Start an engineering design worksheet in your notebook.

2 Place the crackers on top of the paper towel. Build the arch lying down on its side. Using the knife, spread peanut butter on the crackers. Press the crackers lightly together until the arch forms. Will you begin building your arch from one side, both sides, or the center?

3 Carefully tilt your arch up. Does it stand on its own? If not, what can you use to support the arch? Where will you place these supports? What is the engineering term for these supports? Write down your observations in your notebook.

THINK ABOUT IT:
What do you think would happen if these supports cracked?

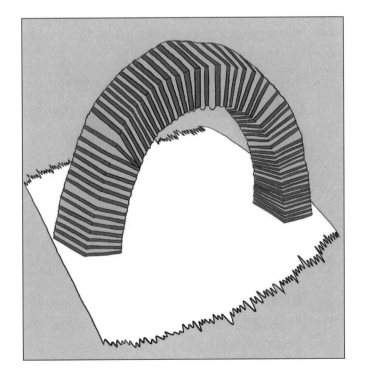

SUPPLIES

* engineering notebook and pencil
* paper towel
* thin crackers
* peanut butter or soy spread
* plastic knife
* assorted erasers, wood blocks, or small containers

PROJECT!

NILOMETER EXPERIMENT

The nilometer helped Egyptian farmers better prepare for a flood or a drought. In this activity, you will create a flood and a drought to study the effect of water on seeds.

1 Fill the containers three-quarters full of soil. Place the containers on the tray. Use a finger to poke a hole in the center of the soil. Place a few seeds in each hole and cover gently with soil. Set to one side.

2 Place the popsicle sticks on a flat surface. With the marker, write one word per stick: Flood, Average, Drought. The words correspond to measurements on the nilometer.

3 Place one popsicle stick in each container. During the next two weeks, follow this schedule.

- **Flood Plant:** Spray with water twice a day.

- **Average Plant:** Allow the soil to dry slightly between watering.

- **Drought Plant:** Do not spray at all.

SUPPLIES

- ✳ 3 clear containers
- ✳ planting soil
- ✳ spade
- ✳ tray
- ✳ fast growing seeds, such as beans
- ✳ popsicle sticks
- ✳ waterproof marker
- ✳ spray bottle with water
- ✳ engineering notebook and pencil

THEN & NOW

THEN: The first canal in the world might have been built by legendary King Menes of Egypt around 4,000 BCE.

NOW: There are plans for a new canal to be built through Nicaragua, but scientists worry how the canal would affect the ecosystem.

WORDS TO KNOW

drought: a long period of dry weather, especially one that damages crops.

76

4 Start a scientific method worksheet. On the first day, write your hypothesis in your notebook. What do you think will happen to your seeds at the end of two weeks? Record your daily observations in your engineering notebook.

5 At the end of two weeks, draw a graph to represent your data. Which plant is healthiest? Why? This site can help you create your graph.

KEYWORD PROMPTS

kids create graph 🔍

THINGS TO THINK ABOUT: Imagine that you are a farmer in ancient Egypt. Based on your experiment, what could you do if the nilometer showed that the Nile was going to flood? What could do you do if the nilometer showed that the water level was low? Write down your ideas in your notebook or brainstorm with a group.

GRAND INGA DAM

The Democratic Republic of Congo (DRC) is the second-largest country in Africa. But less than 10 percent of people in the DRC have electricity. In the future, this may change. There is a plan to build a new dam on the Congo River. If built, the Grand Inga would be the largest hydroelectric power project in the world. It would have 52 turbines that could provide electricity to 40 percent of Africa. Many people do not support the project. Before the project can go ahead, more than 60,000 local residents would have to be moved. Scientists also worry about the environment. They do not know what problems the dam could cause to plants and animals in the area.

THREE GORGES CHALLENGE

SUPPLIES

* large cardboard box lid
* package of small clear hooks and strips or duct tape loops
* scissors
* small empty yogurt container
* string
* engineering notebook and pencil
* pennies

The shiplift at the Three Gorges Dam has four concrete towers. Between the towers is a steel chamber suspended from 256 steel ropes and connected to 128 double-rope pulleys. In this activity, you are going to experiment with pulleys to lift a container of pennies.

1 Lean the large box lid against a wall. Space out the hooks on the lid. You will want some low and some high. Set to one side.

2 Use the sharp end of the scissors to poke a hole on either side of the yogurt container. Thread a piece of string through the holes to make a handle and knot it securely. Lift the container with just your hand to feel how heavy it is.

3 Cut another piece of string about a yard or more in length. Tie one end to the handle of the container. Loop the other end over one of the hooks on your box lid so that the container swings down. You've made a pulley!

PROJECT!

4 Pull on the string. Which direction should the string be pulled? Is it easier or harder to lift the container with the pulley? Why?

5 Start a scientific method worksheet. Do you think looping the thread through another hook will make your job easier? Loop the string through a second hook and test your prediction. Record your observations on a chart.

6 Add pennies to the yogurt cup to make more weight. What can you do to make it easier to lift the heavier container?

Number of Pulleys	Prediction	Result
1		
2		
3		

THINK ABOUT IT: What happens as you add more pulleys? Can you easily lift more weight? Why? What might this mean for larger construction projects?

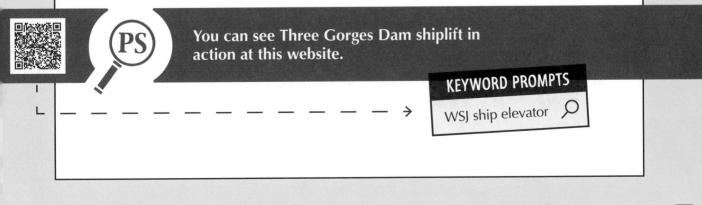

PS You can see Three Gorges Dam shiplift in action at this website.

KEYWORD PROMPTS

WSJ ship elevator

79

PROJECT!

WATER POWER EXPERIMENT

In this activity, you will explore how moving water creates energy.

1 Ask an adult to cut off the top of the bottle, just below the neck. Have an adult help you to use the nail to make a line of six holes around the base of the bottle. At the top of the bottle, make three more holes with the nail.

2 Cut each straw in half. Insert one straw in each hole and secure them with tape.

3 Cut four lengths of string. Tie a piece of string to each hole at the top of the bottle. Gather the strings together and secure them with a knot. Attach the fourth piece of string to this knot. It will be your handle.

4 What will happen when you pour water into the bottle? Form a hypothesis and write it down in a scientific method worksheet in your notebook.

5 Hold the bottle over a sink. Pour water into the bottle. What happens? Record the results in your journal.

THINK ABOUT IT: The force of the water makes the bottle spin just as the energy from water makes a turbine spin to create electricity. If you pour water into the bottle at different rates, what happens? Can you make the bottle turn slower and faster by changing the way you pour?

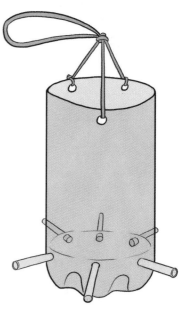

SUPPLIES

* 1-liter empty plastic bottle
* scissors
* nail
* 3 straws
* tape
* string
* engineering notebook and pencil

80

BUILD A WATERWHEEL

Before there were hydroelectric power plants, people harnessed the energy of moving water using waterwheels. For example, waterwheels moved machinery within a mill for grinding grain. Try making your own waterwheel and see if you can find a job for your creation!

SUPPLIES

* ✳ scissors
* ✳ disposable coffee cup lid
* ✳ bamboo skewer
* ✳ 4–6 recycled coffee pods or bottle caps, etc.
* ✳ duct tape
* ✳ 2 large disposable cups
* ✳ engineering notebook and pencil

1 With an adult, carefully use the scissors to make a hole in the center of the lid. It needs to be slightly larger than the skewer. Push the bamboo skewer through the center of the lid.

2 Tape the recycled coffee pods around the lid. They should all face in the same direction. This is your waterwheel.

3 Turn the cups upside down to form two towers. Carefully push a cup into either side of the skewer.

4 Place the waterwheel in a sink. What will happen when you pour water on your wheel? Record your hypothesis in a scientific method worksheet and then try it! What do you observe?

THINGS TO TRY: Will pouring the water from different heights change your results? Test your experiment. Write down what you see in your engineering notebook. Looking at your data, why do you think hydropower plants are built on rivers with a sharp drop such as a waterfall?

SUPPLIES

✳ this book
✳ pencil

WORD GAME ACTIVITY

Use as many words as you can from this book to fill in the blanks. Share your silly story with a friend.

- **noun:** a person, place, or thing
- **plural noun:** more than one person, place, or thing
- **adjective:** a word that describes a noun

- **verb:** an action word
- **adverb:** a word that describes a verb

_____'s Canal Adventure
<small>YOUR NAME</small>

Yesterday, I went on a _____ canal adventure with my best-friend
<small>ADJECTIVE</small>
_____. It took us through _____ and _____ as far as my eyes could
<small>FRIEND'S NAME</small> <small>NOUN</small> <small>NOUN</small>
see. The canal had once been used to move _____ and _____, the guide
<small>NOUN</small> <small>NOUN</small>
said. I wondered how many _____ it had taken to _____ the canal.
<small>PLURAL NOUN</small> <small>VERB</small>
They must have _____ so _____, I thought.
<small>VERB</small> <small>ADVERB</small>

The _____ sun shone _____ as we cruised all the way to a _____. From
<small>ADJECTIVE</small> <small>ADVERB</small> <small>NOUN</small>
the deck of the _____ boat, I could see two _____. My best friend
<small>ADJECTIVE</small> <small>PLURAL NOUN</small>
_____ and I decided to explore the _____. But when we stepped off
<small>FRIEND'S NAME</small> <small>NOUN</small>
the boat, a _____ fog came out of nowhere. Then, we heard a _____
<small>ADJECTIVE</small> <small>ADJECTIVE</small>
voice. A man wearing a _____ handed us two shovels and we were told to
<small>NOUN</small>
get digging! Beads of sweat _____ from my brow. "We have to get out of
<small>VERB</small>
here," I told my friend. When the man left, we _____ our shovels and
<small>VERB</small>
_____ to where we last saw the boat. That's when the _____ fog
<small>VERB</small> <small>ADJECTIVE</small>
surrounded us again. When it lifted, we were back at the _____. "Where
<small>ADJECTIVE</small>
will this canal lead us next" I wondered.

ancestor: someone from your family or culture who lived before you.

aqueduct: a bridge that carries water over an obstacle.

aquifer: an underground layer of water-filled rock.

arch: a curved structure in the shape of an upside-down U.

Archimedes screw: a device with a spiral used to raise water.

atmosphere: the blanket of gases around the earth.

BCE: put after a date, BCE stands for Before Common Era and counts years down to zero. CE stands for Common Era and counts years up from zero. This book was published in 2018 CE.

beam: a strong horizontal structure that provides support.

bedrock: solid rock beneath soil and gravel.

buttress: a support used to strengthen a structure.

canal: a manmade channel used to deliver water.

canyon: a deep, narrow valley with steep sides.

capstan: an upright cylinder that turns to wind a rope or cable.

civil engineering: a branch of engineering that deals with designing structures such as dams, canals, tunnels, or bridges.

cofferdam: a temporary structure used to keep a construction site dry.

collapse: to fall in or down suddenly.

Colonial America: the name given to America during the years 1607–1776, when new settlers came from Europe and before the United States became its own country.

concrete: a hard material for construction made with cement, sand, and water.

condense: when a gas cools down and changes into a liquid.

continent: one of seven large landmasses in the world.

convex: a rounded shape like the outside of a bowl.

current: the steady flow of water in one direction.

dam: a wall, usually built across moving water, to hold some of it back.

debris: the remains of something, such as dirt, rocks, and vegetation.

GLOSSARY

diversion tunnel: a tunnel built to redirect a portion of a river.

downstream: farther down a river in the direction a river or stream flows.

dredge: to scoop out the weeds and mud from a waterway, such as a canal.

drought: a long period of dry weather, especially one that damages crops.

dynasty: a powerful family or group that rules for many years.

ecosystem: a community of animals and plants existing and interacting together.

embankment: a wall of earth or stone.

engineer: someone who uses science, math, and creativity to solve problems.

engineering: using science, math, and creativity to design and build things.

environment: the natural world in which people, animals, and plants live.

erosion: the gradual wearing away of rock or soil by water and wind.

evaporate: to change from a liquid to a gas, or vapor.

extinct: when a species dies out and there are no more left in the world.

famine: a severe food shortage.

fertile: describes soil that is good for growing crops.

fertilizer: to add something to soil to make crops grow better.

fish ladder: a series of pools that allow fish to swim around a dam.

flood: when the water in a river or lake overflows.

force: a push or a pull that causes a change of motion in an object.

freshwater: water that is not salty.

geometric: straight lines or simple shapes such as circles or squares.

glacier: an enormous mass of ice and snow that moves slowly with the pull of gravity.

GPS: stands for global positioning system, which is the system of navigation satellites that orbit Earth.

gondola: a small, narrow boat made to move with a single oar.

gorge: a deep, narrow passage.

gravity: a force that pulls objects to the earth.

groundwater: water that is underground in spaces between rocks.

hydroelectric power: energy generated by the flow of water.

immigrant: a person who comes to settle in a new country.

irrigation: moving water through canals, ditches, or tunnels to water crops.

isthmus: a narrow strip of land with sea on both sides.

landslide: the movement of rock or earth down a slope.

legging: people using their feet to push against a tunnel wall to propel a boat.

lever: a bar that rests on a support and lifts or moves things.

lock: an engineering feature on canals that helps raise or lower boats from one level of water to another.

Mesopotamia: a region of the Middle East that today is part of Iraq.

miter gate: a lock gate that, when closed, forms a V shape pointing upstream.

navigation: planning or following a route.

nutrients: substances that living things need to live and grow.

penstock: a pipe that leads to a turbine.

pound lock: a chamber with gates at both ends to control water levels in the pound.

pressure: a force that pushes on an object.

prototype: a model of something that allows engineers to test their ideas.

pulley: a wheel with a groove for a rope used to lift a load.

reinforced: made stronger.

reservoir: an artificial lake used for storing water.

riprap: chunks of stone used to prevent erosion.

runoff: water that flows off the land into bodies of water.

shaduf: an ancient water-lifting device for irrigation.

shiplift: a platform that is used to lift ships out of the water and put them back in.

silt: fine-grained soil rich in nutrients, often found at the bottom of rivers or lakes.

simple machine: a tool that uses one movement to complete work.

species: a group of plants or animals that are related and look like each other.

spillway: a channel that takes water away from the dam.

structure: something that is built, such as a building, bridge, or tunnel.

towpath: a path along a canal traveled by horses pulling boats.

trade: the exchange of goods for other goods or money.

trapezoid: a four-sided shape with at least two parallel sides.

turbine: a machine with blades turned by the force of water, air, or steam.

upstream: the direction opposite to the flow of a stream or river.

valve: a structure that controls the passage of fluid.

vertical: straight up and down.

volume: the amount of space an object takes up.

water cycle: the continuous movement of water from the earth to the clouds and back to the earth again.

watershed: the area of land that drains into a river or a lake.

water vapor: water as a gas, such as fog, steam, or mist.

windlass: a device that uses a rope wound around a barrel to raise objects.

METRIC CONVERSIONS

Use this chart to find the metric equivalents to the English measurements in this book. If you need to know a half measurement, divide by two. If you need to know twice the measurement, multiply by two. How do you find a quarter measurement? How do you find three times the measurement?

English	Metric
1 inch	2.5 centimeters
1 foot	30.5 centimeters
1 yard	0.9 meter
1 mile	1.6 kilometers
1 pound	0.5 kilogram
1 teaspoon	5 milliliters
1 tablespoon	15 milliliters
1 cup	237 milliliters

WEBSITES

BBC: Architectural Styles Across Britain, Canals
bbc.co.uk/history/british/gallery_buildingstyles_05.shtml

PBS Learning Material: Building the Erie Canal
pbslearningmedia.org/resource/adlit08.ush.exp.erie/
building-the-erie-canal/#.WUl2_mjytPY

Ducksters: U.S. History, Erie Canal
ducksters.com/history/us_1800s/erie_canal.php

U.S. Energy Information Administration: Energy Kids
eia.gov/kids/energy.cfm?page=hydropower_home-basics

Engineer Girl: engineergirl.org

Foundation for Water and Energy Education: Walk through a Hydroelectric Project
fwee.org/nw-hydro-tours/walk-through-a-hydroelectric-project

PBS American Experience: Grand Coulee Dam
pbs.org/wgbh/americanexperience/films/coulee

Idaho Public Television: Science Trek, Dam Facts
idahoptv.org/sciencetrek/topics/dams/facts.cfm

National Geographic:
Hoover Dam: vimeo.com/223914946
Panama Canal: natgeotv.com/asia/big-bigger-biggest/videos/panama-canal-locks
Three Gorges Dam: natgeotv.com/za/lost-in-china/videos/three-gorges-dam

PBS American Experience: Panama Canal
pbs.org/wgbh/americanexperience/films/panama

PBS Building Big: Dams
pbs.org/wgbh/buildingbig/dam

Science Channel: Panama Canal
sciencechannel.com/tv-shows/impossible-engineering/impossible-engineering-videos/
the-epic-engineering-of-the-panama-canal-overhaul

Smithsonian Institute:
sil.si.edu/Exhibitions/Make-the-Dirt-Fly/blast-1.htm

Tennessee Valley Authority: How Electricity Is Made
tvakids.com/river/aboutdams.htm

RESOURCES

BOOKS

Caney, Steven. *Steven Caney's Ultimate Building Book*. Running Press Kids, 2006.

Graham, Ian. *You Wouldn't Want to Work on the Hoover Dam!: An Explosive Job You'd Rather Not Do*. Franklin Watts, 2012.

Halls, Kelly Milner. *The Story of the Hoover Dam: A History Perspectives Book*. Cherry Lake Publishing, 2014.

Pascal, Janet. *What Is the Panama Canal?* Grosset & Dunlap: Paw Prints, 2014.

Latham, Donna. *Canals and Dams: Investigate Feats of Engineering*. Nomad Press, 2013.

Mann, Elizabeth. *Hoover Dam: The Story of Hard Times, Tough People and the Taming of a Wild River*. Mikaya Press, 2006.

Ringstad, Arnold. *The Building of the Hoover Dam*. The Childs World Inc., 2017.

Stefoff, Rebecca. *The Panama Canal*. Raintree, 2016.

Weil, Ann. *The World's Most Amazing Dams*. Raintree, 2013.

Zuehlke, Jeffrey. *The Hoover Dam*. Lerner Publications Co., 2009.

QR CODE GLOSSARY

Page 5: youtube.com/watch?v=t40z21ZtVq0

Page 18: youtube.com/watch?v=ouxc_WUcNOw

Page 26: youtube.com/watch?v=5NIPil7NDDk

Page 41: youtube.com/watch?v=0IsqAejuaBw

Page 42: washingtonpost.com/videonational/drone-video-shows-iconic-glory-hole-spillway-overflowing/2017/02/21/109aa4a6-f883-11e6-aa1e-5f735ee31334_video.html?utm_term=.18d722576c8d

Page 51: earthobservatory.nasa.gov/IOTD/view.php?id=85900

Page 77: nces.ed.gov/nceskids/graphing/classic/bar.asp

Page 79: wsj.com/video/worlds-largest-ship-elevator-opens-in-china/7EC1CE0F-8006-40D2-BAF3-435999C2DFAA.html

ESSENTIAL QUESTIONS

Introduction: What problem do you see that you would like to fix? What can you invent to solve it?

Chapter 1: How are canals and dams connected to the world's water supply?

Chapter 2: What structures do dams and canals have in common?

Chapter 3: What shapes are used to give dams strength?

Chapter 4: How do locks improve trade and navigation?

Chapter 5: How are the dams and canals being built today different from those built in the past?